Inclined Planes

by Joanne Mattern

BLASTOFF! READERS
2

Note to Librarians, Teachers, and Parents:

Blastoff! Readers are carefully developed by literacy experts and combine standards-based content with developmentally appropriate text.

Level 1 provides the most support through repetition of high-frequency words, light text, predictable sentence patterns, and strong visual support.

Level 2 offers early readers a bit more challenge through varied simple sentences, increased text load, and less repetition of high-frequency words.

Level 3 advances early-fluent readers toward fluency through increased text and concept load, less reliance on visuals, longer sentences, and more literary language.

Level 4 builds reading stamina by providing more text per page, increased use of punctuation, greater variation in sentence patterns, and increasingly challenging vocabulary.

Level 5 encourages children to move from "learning to read" to "reading to learn" by providing even more text, varied writing styles, and less familiar topics.

Whichever book is right for your reader, Blastoff! Readers are the perfect books to build confidence and encourage a love of reading that will last a lifetime!

This edition first published in 2020 by Bellwether Media, Inc.

No part of this publication may be reproduced in whole or in part without written permission of the publisher. For information regarding permission, write to Bellwether Media, Inc., Attention: Permissions Department, 6012 Blue Circle Drive, Minnetonka, MN 55343.

Library of Congress Cataloging-in-Publication Data

Names: Mattern, Joanne, 1963- author.
Title: Inclined Planes / by Joanne Mattern.
Description: Minneapolis, MN : Bellwether Media, Inc., 2020. | Series: Blastoff! Readers: Simple Machines Fun! |
    Includes bibliographical references and index. | Audience: 5-8. | Audience: K to grade 3.
Identifiers: LCCN 2018056033 (print) | LCCN 2018060222 (ebook) | ISBN 9781618915313 (ebook) |
    ISBN 9781626179912 (hardcover : alk. paper)
Subjects: LCSH: Inclined planes--Juvenile literature.
Classification: LCC TJ1428 (ebook) | LCC TJ1428 .M38 2020 (print) | DDC 621.8--dc23
LC record available at https://lccn.loc.gov/2018056033

Editor: Christina Leaf   Designer: Jeffrey Kollock

Printed in the United States of America, North Mankato, MN.

Table of Contents

What Are Inclined Planes?

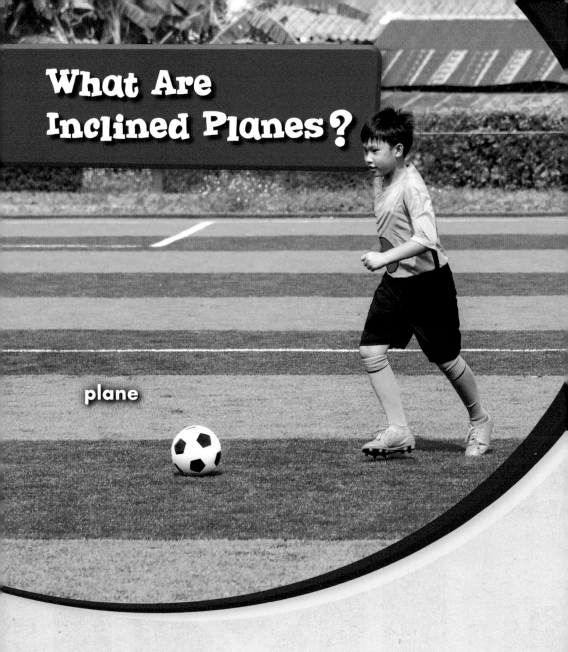

plane

A plane is a flat surface.

Inclined planes are higher on one end than the other. They are also called ramps.

You can push or roll things up or down an inclined plane. This is easier than lifting them.

For example, you can roll
a wheelchair up a ramp.

How Do Inclined Planes Work?

It takes a lot of **force** to lift a heavy object.

Pushing it up a ramp takes less force. The ramp holds some of the weight.

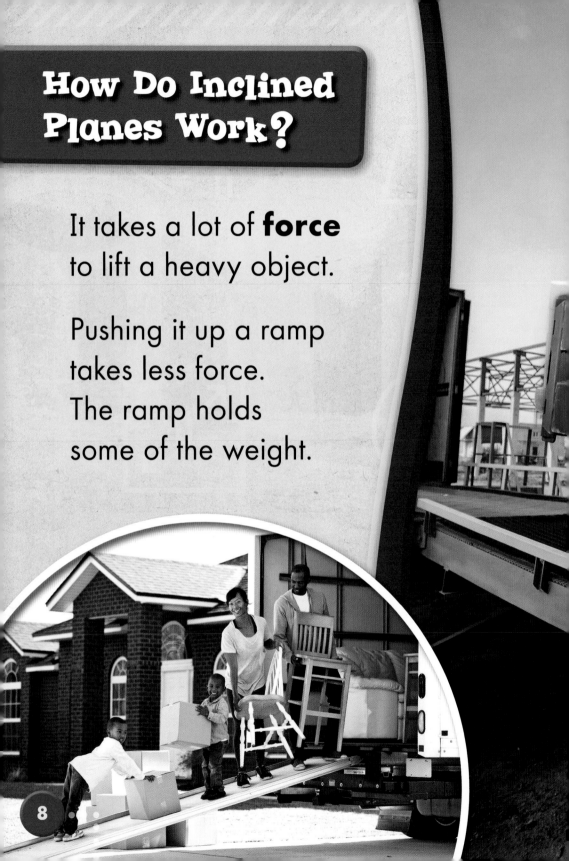

An inclined plane spreads the force over a longer **distance**. The object is pushed farther but with less force.

How Inclined Planes Work

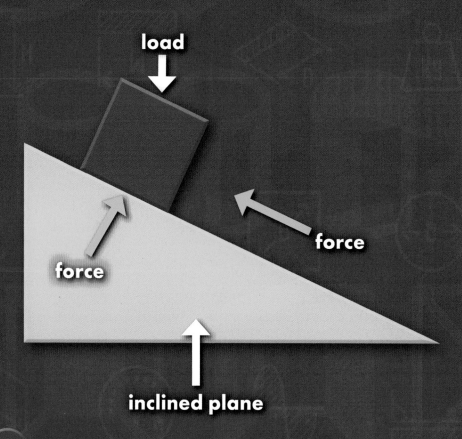

load

force

force

inclined plane

Slope changes the force
needed. Low slopes do
not need much force.

It is harder to push something up a **steep** slope. **Gravity** pulls harder on objects on steep slopes.

steep slope

Force and Inclined Planes

What You Need :

- a small bag of rice or beans
- a rubber band
- a ruler
- a stack of books
- a small board

What To Do :

1. Cut the rubber band. Tie it around the top of the bag.

2. Lay the board against the books to make an inclined plane.

3. Lift the bag by the rubber band onto the books. Measure how far the rubber band stretches as you lift. This shows the force it takes to lift the bag.

4. Now use the rubber band to pull the bag up the inclined plane. As you pull, measure how far the rubber band stretches. Does it need more or less force?

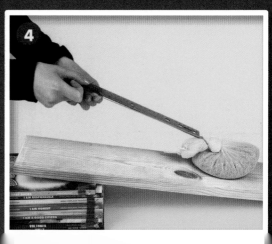

Inclined Planes in Our Lives

The **ancient** Egyptians may have used inclined planes to build the pyramids.

They pushed heavy blocks up ramps.

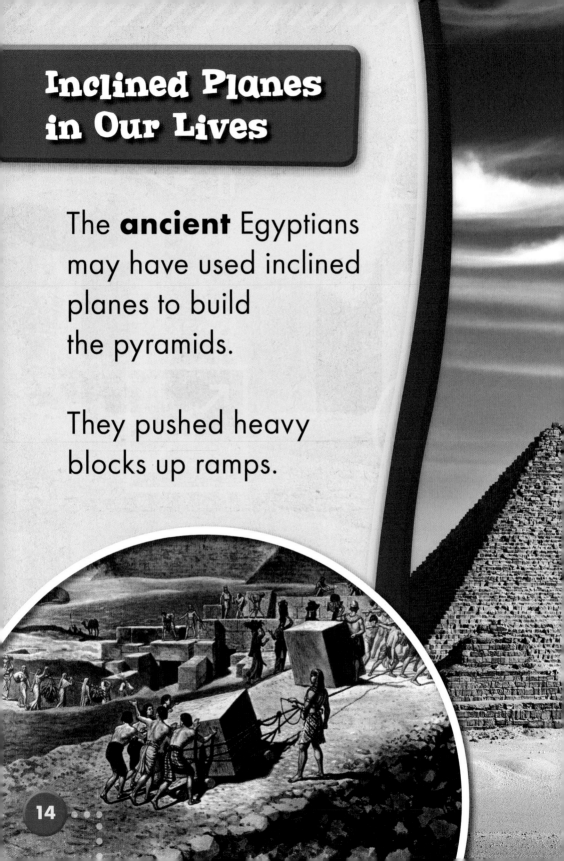

Pyramids
of Giza

Today we use inclined
planes in many ways.
Stairs are inclined planes.

Ramps and slides are, too.

Build a Ramp

- a heavy can
- a short stack of books
- a small board

What To Do :

1. Lift the can from the floor to the top of the stack of books.

2. Place the board against the stack to create a ramp. Roll the can up the ramp. Is this easier than lifting it?

highway ramp

Roads also have inclined planes. Highway ramps carry cars up or down to other roads.

An inclined plane can be part of a **complex machine**. A cable car uses **pulleys** and inclined planes to go up mountains.

Everyday Inclined Planes

Simple

slides

stairs

Complex

escalator

tow rope

Inclined planes make our work easier every day!

Glossary

ancient—from long ago

complex machine—a machine that combines two or more simple machines

distance—the space between things

force—the amount of energy it takes to do something

gravity—the force that attracts an object downward, toward the center of the earth

pulleys—simple machines that use rope and a wheel and axle to make objects easier to lift

slope—how much an inclined plane rises or falls

steep—rising or falling sharply

To Learn More

AT THE LIBRARY

Oxlade, Chris. *Making Machines with Ramps and Wedges*. Chicago, Ill.: Heinemann Raintree, 2015.

Rivera, Andrea. *Inclined Planes*. Minneapolis, Minn.: Abdo Zoom, 2017.

Weakland, Mark. *Fred Flintstone's Adventures with Inclined Planes: A Rampin' Good Time!*. North Mankato, Minn.: Capstone Press, 2016.

ON THE WEB

FACTSURFER

Factsurfer.com gives you a safe, fun way to find more information.

1. Go to www.factsurfer.com.

2. Enter "inclined planes" into the search box and click 🔍.

3. Select your book cover to see a list of related web sites.

Index

The images in this book are reproduced through the courtesy of: Wisanu_nuu, front cover; Kdonmuang, pp. 4-5, MilanB, p. 5; yanik88, p. 6; fotosparrow, pp. 6-7; kali9, p. 8; Andrei Mayatnik, pp. 8-9; kavalenkau, pp. 10-11; Vixit, p. 12; Bellwether Media, pp. 13 (all), 18 (all); Classic Stock/ Alamy, p. 14; WitR, pp. 14-15; S-F, pp. 16-17; Mia2you, p. 17; Kekyalyaynen, p. 19; Elena Yakusheva, pp. 20-21; Piotr Wawrzyniuk, p. 21 (slide); dailin, p. 21 (stairs); Maltsev Semion, p. 21 (escalator); Photobac, p. 21 (tow rope).